My Silly Book of
OPPOSITES

Written by Susan Amerikaner
Illustrated by Judy Ziegler

SILVER PRESS

Amerikaner, Susan.
    My silly book of opposites / by Susan
Amerikaner; illustrated by Judy Ziegler.
        p.   cm.
    Summary: Introduces the concept of oppo-
sites through the adventures of two friends,
Bunny and Hippo.
    1. English language—Synonyms and
antonyms—Juvenile literature. [1. English
language—Synonyms and antonyms.]   I.
Ziegler, Judy, ill.   II. Title.
PE1591.A54   1989
428.1—dc19   89-5984
ISBN 0-671-68122-2   CIP
ISBN 0-671-68366-7 (lib. bdg.)   AC
ISBN 382-24675-6 (pbk)

Published by Silver Press, a division of
Silver Burdett Press, Inc.,
Simon & Schuster, Inc.,
Prentice Hall Bldg., Englewood Cliffs, NJ 07632.
Printed in the United States of America.

10 9 8 7 6 5 4 3 2

A Note to Parents

MY SILLY BOOKS are perfect for parents and children to share together. Each book is designed to introduce a beginning concept. Read each one first, just for fun. Encourage your child to look carefully. The illustrations contain additional details that reinforce concepts. Large, simple text encourages your preschool child to pick out words.

Now, look again–there's more to be found in the silly animal antics. Ask your child to think about what might come next. Be imaginative! Encourage your child to be creative and, most of all, have fun!

little

Bunny and Hippo are friends.
Bunny is little.

big

Hippo is big.

over

Bunny hops over a fence.

under

Hippo gets stuck under the fence.

pushes

Bunny pushes.

pulls

Bunny pulls.

in

Bunny digs a big hole.
Hippo falls in.

out

Hippo climbs out.

leads

"What a lot of work!" says Hippo.
"Now I'm hungry. Let's have lunch."
Hippo leads the way.

follows

Bunny follows.

open

The door is open.

The door is closed.
Oops! Poor Hippo!

long

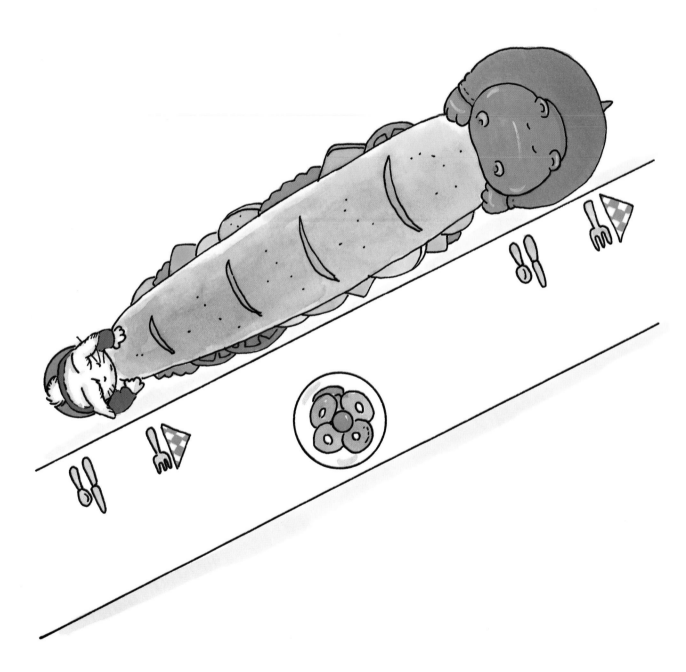

Bunny and Hippo share a long sandwich.

short

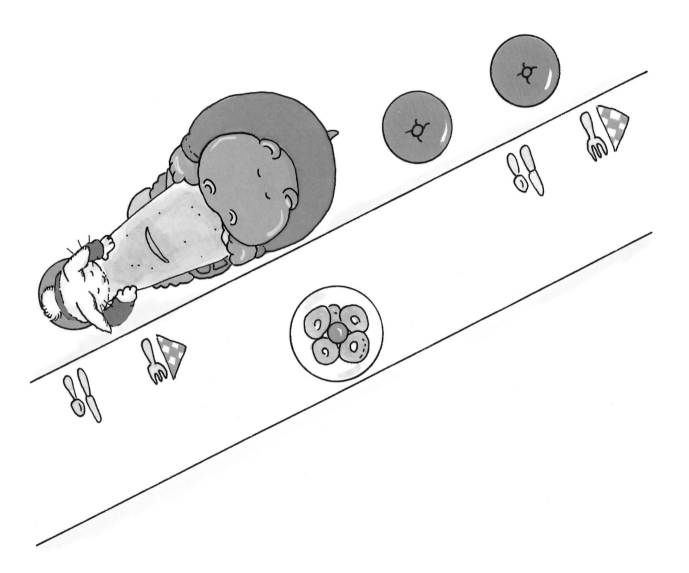

Now the sandwich is short.

empty

Bunny's belly is empty, but...

full

Hippo's belly is full.

up

"I think we need some exercise," says Hippo.
Bunny skates up the hill.

down

Hippo skates down the hill.

fast

Bunny is fast.

slow

Hippo is slow.

stops

Bunny stops.

goes

Hippo goes.

wet

Splash! Poor Hippo!
Hippo is wet.

dry

Bunny is dry.

hot

Bunny builds a fire.
The fire is hot.

Hippo is cold,
but Hippo will soon be warm.

day

"Thanks, Bunny!" says Hippo.
"What a day we have had!"

Soon it is night.
The two friends are sleepy.

Bunny curls up in a ball.
"A little friend can sure be
a big help!" says Hippo.

Stone Arch Readers are designed to provide enjoyable reading experiences, as well as opportunities to develop vocabulary, literacy skills, and comprehension. Here are a few ways to support your beginning reader:

• Talk with your child about the ideas addressed in the story.

• Discuss each illustration, mentioning the characters, where they are, and what they are doing.

• Read with expression, pointing to each word. You may want to read the whole story through and then revisit parts of the story to ensure that the meanings of words or phrases are understood.

• Talk about why the character did what he or she did and what your child would do in that situation.

• Help your child connect with characters and events in the story.

Remember, reading with your child should be fun, not forced. Each moment spent reading with your child is a priceless investment in his or her literacy life.

Gail Saunders-Smith, Ph.D.

floor section

8 × 14"

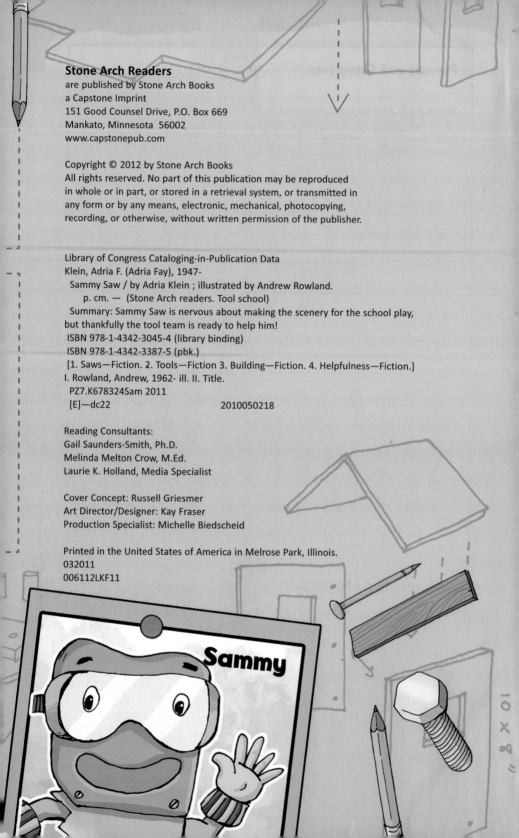

Stone Arch Readers

are published by Stone Arch Books
a Capstone Imprint
151 Good Counsel Drive, P.O. Box 669
Mankato, Minnesota 56002
www.capstonepub.com

Library of Congress Cataloging-in-Publication Data
Klein, Adria F. (Adria Fay), 1947-
  Sammy Saw / by Adria Klein ; illustrated by Andrew Rowland.
     p. cm. — (Stone Arch readers. Tool school)
  Summary: Sammy Saw is nervous about making the scenery for the school play,
but thankfully the tool team is ready to help him!
  ISBN 978-1-4342-3045-4 (library binding)
  ISBN 978-1-4342-3387-5 (pbk.)
  [1. Saws—Fiction. 2. Tools—Fiction 3. Building—Fiction. 4. Helpfulness—Fiction.]
  I. Rowland, Andrew, 1962- ill. II. Title.
   PZ7.K678324Sam 2011
   [E]—dc22   2010050218

Reading Consultants:
Gail Saunders-Smith, Ph.D.
Melinda Melton Crow, M.Ed.
Laurie K. Holland, Media Specialist

Cover Concept: Russell Griesmer
Art Director/Designer: Kay Fraser
Production Specialist: Michelle Biedscheid

Printed in the United States of America in Melrose Park, Illinois.
032011
006112LKF11

Sammy